IMAGES
of America

CUYAHOGA VALLEY

On the cover: The first Boston Township/Peninsula Village Home Coming was held in 1916. These events were usually held at the Boston Township Hall on the northeast corner of Riverview Road and Route 303. The cover photograph shows a group assembled for the 1939 Home Coming. By 1959, these get-togethers waned with the fading of Fauble Post 543 of the American Legion. As a project of the United States Bicentennial, in 1976, this event was resurrected as Home Days. It was held at the school on Bronson Avenue until insurance liability issues ended the fun in the mid-1980s. *(PLHS)*

IMAGES
of America

CUYAHOGA VALLEY

Cuyahoga Valley Historical Museum
Cuyahoga Valley National Park Association

ARCADIA
PUBLISHING

Published by Arcadia Publishing
Charleston, South Carolina

Library of Congress Catalog Card Number: 2003116954

For all general information contact Arcadia Publishing at:
Telephone 843-853-2070
Fax 843-853-0044
E-mail sales@arcadiapublishing.com
For customer service and orders:
Toll-Free 1-888-313-2665

Visit us on the Internet at www.arcadiapublishing.com

 Cuyahoga
Valley
Historical
Museum

 Cuyahoga Valley
National Park
Association

CONTENTS

ACKNOWLEDGMENTS

We wish to express our appreciation to the following organizations and individuals for the use of their images in this publication. Without their assistance we would not have been able to present such a well-rounded pictorial history of the Cuyahoga Valley.

Photo credits are noted with each image. For the purpose of brevity, we have abbreviated the following organizations' names:

Bedford Historical Society	(BHS)
Cleveland Metroparks	(CMP)
Cuyahoga Valley National Park	(CVNP)
First Bedford United Methodist Church	(FUMCB)
Girl Scouts of Western Reserve Council, Inc.	(GSWRC)
Jet Lowe, Historic American Engineering Survey	(HAER)
Peninsula Library and Historical Society	(PLHS)
Phillis Wheatley Association of Cleveland	(PWA)

Robert J. Botzum
Tom Jones
R. Todd Mayer
Kathleen Schnell
Nina Stanford
Dale Wagner
Gerald Wuchter

We would also like to thank Dan Liddle for all his work scanning the images for this publication.

The Cuyahoga Valley Historical Museum and Cuyahoga Valley National Park Association hope you will enjoy this publication.

Melissa Arnold
Randy Bergdorf
Sam Tamburro

INTRODUCTION

The story of the Cuyahoga Valley can be told through its people and landscapes. The valley's landscape has evolved greatly over time. Starting as a wilderness inhabited by nomadic people, the valley changed into scattered agrarian townships during the early 19th century. Gradually, a landscape of small villages mingled with isolated industrial uses evolved. As the rural landscape adopted a more "suburban" atmosphere, the valley became a center for recreational activities. While traces of its diverse past remain, today the valley is predominantly a recreational landscape.

One way to communicate the valley's multi-layered history through these historical images is by organizing this book as if one were traveling the valley from the north, beginning at what is today Thornburg Station and ending south at the intersection of Bath and Riverview Roads, where once there existed the town of Botzum.

Each community in this valley developed much like one another, each benefiting from the river, canal, and railroad. However, each has a different story to tell that is shaped by the people who have resided there throughout the years.

The Cuyahoga Valley is a 22-mile river valley in northeast Ohio, nestled between Akron and Cleveland, on land once known as the Connecticut Western Reserve. This valley was fashioned as the glaciers moved across it and receded, sculpting its steep walls and ravines. As the great sheets of ice moved, they deposited a mixture of clay, silt, sand and gravel. In addition to these numerous natural resources, the area was heavily forested with Beech, Elm, Hickory, Maple, Oak, and Walnut. Furthermore, many varieties of nuts and berries such as chestnuts, walnuts, strawberries, blackberries, currants, and wild cherries grew in abundance. These resources would serve all of the peoples who would inhabit this valley.

Following the departure of the glaciers, the first peoples to inhabit the valley were the pre-historic Paleo-Indians and numerous Native American tribes. In the beginning, most of these tribes were nomadic and followed the herds of animals that roamed the valley. They later built villages, but eventually they were displaced by settlers from the east.

European settlement in the Cuyahoga Valley was a direct result of events that happened centuries earlier. When Connecticut was given its royal charter, the language included all lands from coast to coast. After the American Revolution, the struggling new government desired to end territorial disputes. In the 1700s four states laid claim to lands laying to the west of Pennsylvania: New York, Virginia, Massachusetts, and Connecticut. All of these states ceded their claims to the lands. Connecticut, in 1796, was the last to cede her western territory;

however, she "reserved" a strip of territory along the south shore of Lake Erie stretching 120 miles west from Pennsylvania with a southern boundary at the 41st parallel. This area, a total of three million acres, became known as the Connecticut Western Reserve. A group of thirty-five speculators was created, and they became known as the Connecticut Land Company. The company purchased most of this region for re-sale to investors and settlers.

In 1796, Connecticut sent a group of men to begin surveying only the lands east of the Cuyahoga River into townships five miles square. According to the Treaty of Greenville, which was negotiated in 1795, the Native Americans ceded their eastern lands to the United States. It was another ten years before the lands to the west were opened for surveying and settlement. In 1805, the Treaty of Fort Industry was negotiated and the western lands were made available for surveying. Settlement was slow due to topographical obstacles, steep valley walls, dense forests, and isolation to outside markets. But these obstacles did not impede the settlers from New England. They had "Ohio Fever" and traveled many miles from their well-established homes and towns in New England to this dense wilderness. Here, they began to clear the thick forest for planting crops and chop out areas in which to build suitable dwellings. In spite of the availability of natural resources, their primary occupation was subsistence farming of corn, wheat, and rye. Common farm stock consisted of oxen, horses, and razor back hogs. The hogs furnished lard for the household, and their hide was made into shoe leather. Although the farms progressed, the settlers faced three major economic problems: the scarcity of labor, the lack of capital, and isolation from the eastern markets. To get goods from this interior, a transportation system would be needed to link it to the outside world.

In 1825, The Ohio Legislature authorized the construction of the Ohio & Erie Canal from Cleveland to Portsmouth. From Cleveland, the canal ran south along the Cuyahoga River, across the Portage Summit, along the Tuscarawas River, eventually to the Scioto at Columbus, and south to the town of Portsmouth on the Ohio River. It was over 300 miles in length. The dedication ceremonies for the Akron-to-Cleveland section were held on July 4, 1827. The valley was finally linked to markets in the south and east. Subsistence farming gave way to cash-crop farming, living conditions improved, and more settlers arrived. The communities of Boston, Peninsula, Everett, Ira, and Botzum sprang up along the canal, and although they were primarily agrarian in nature, industries were beginning to develop as a result of the opening of the canal. Industries such as canal boat building, milling, quarrying, and brick making soon appeared.

During the first three quarters of the 19th century, the valley's dominant transportation system was the Ohio & Erie Canal, but in 1880, another mode of transportation appeared in the form of the Valley Railway, which became the Cleveland Terminal & Valley Railroad and eventually the Baltimore & Ohio Railroad. Its route paralleled the banks of the Cuyahoga River and the Ohio & Erie Canal. Stations were built in Brecksville, Independence, Boston, Peninsula, Everett, Ira, and Botzum. Goods were now shipped faster and more economically by rail. Although the canal still shipped wood and coal, the valley farmers relied on the rail line to get their perishable items to markets more quickly. The railway not only brought goods but also visitors from the nearby cities of Akron and Cleveland who were looking to escape the noisy, overcrowded cities for recreational opportunities in this pastoral setting.

Life in the valley changed drastically after it suffered a great natural disaster, the great Flood of 1913. Valley communities were devastated. Houses and shops were completely destroyed or were left uninhabitable. The Valley Railway suffered extensive damage. It was three months before rail service was restored and valley residents finally received their mail, newspapers, and supplies. Cleanup and repair was slow, and life eventually returned to normal in the valley. However, the flood damaged the Ohio & Erie Canal beyond repair. Farming remained during the 20th century; however, farmsteads decreased in acreage and crops were diversified to meet the needs of growing urban markets in Cleveland and Akron.

By the early 20th century, the Cuyahoga Valley was already being recognized for its recreational potential. As a result, both Akron and Cleveland Metropolitan Parks Districts eventually used sections of the valley as park space with the assistance of the Civilian

Conservation Corps (CCC) in the 1930s. The CCC helped to build parks such as Virginia Kendall, Brecksville, and Furnace Run Reservation and created a recreational cultural landscape that is still evident today.

On December 27, 1974, Cuyahoga Valley National Park was established. Today, visitors enjoy numerous types of recreational activities surrounded by the valley's natural beauty. It can be difficult for visitors to envision the existence of these once thriving 19th century communities. Over time, the pastoral landscape is being reclaimed by dense forest. Through the images in this book, the peoples, towns, and the lost landscapes can be revisited.

This *c.* 1900 photograph depicts the three modes of transportation through the Cuyahoga Valley; The Ohio & Erie Canal (far left), the Cuyahoga River (center), and the Valley Railroad (right). (*PLHS*)

One

TRAVELING FROM
THORNBURG TO JAITE

The northern extent of the Cuyahoga Valley contains a varied historical landscape, some of which was captured in historic photographs. As early as the 1870s, "shutterbugs" chronicled distinct features wrought by geography, settlement patterns, and evolving transportation systems. Their photographs illustrate a common landscape and provide small glimpses into everyday life in the valley.

The northern part of the Cuyahoga Valley experienced some of the earliest Euro-American settlement in the region. From 1786 to 1787, a group of Moravian missionaries and approximately 100 Native American converts created a temporary settlement near the confluence of Tinker's Creek and the Cuyahoga River. The settlement, called Pilgerruh, or Pilgrim's Rest, was located on the site of a former Ottawa Indian village. From the Moravians' recorded accounts, the floodplain proved to be fertile for their short stay. It is this bountiful valley that would attract the first permanent settlers in the early 19th century.

As the 19th century emerged, small subsistence farms dotted the landscape in the northern section of the Cuyahoga Valley. This semi-isolated lifestyle was similar to other frontier settlements throughout the new state of Ohio. However, the construction of the Ohio & Erie Canal would forever change the landscape and everyday life in the valley. By 1825, hundreds of immigrant and migrant laborers flooded into the valley to build the canal. Tons of dirt and sandstone were excavated and quarried to build locks, waste weirs, floodgates, and other structures associated with the new system.

Changes in the economy brought on by the canal were equally dramatic. Now connected to other regional markets, the Cuyahoga Valley was part of a transportation system that helped to create a national economy in the United States. Farms and commercial operations sprang up along Canal Road to establish close proximity to the new transportation artery. Farmhouses like Stephen Frazee's and Edmund Gleeson's still stand along Canal Road as reminders of the legacy of the canal on the valley's agricultural community.

In 1855, Robert and Andrew Alexander built their grist mill at Lock 37 and utilized the hydraulic power created by a waste weir along the southeast side of the lock. The mill became a destination for area wheat farmers. The mill processed flour and shipped it to eastern markets. The mill continued to mill grain well into the 20th century even after the Ohio & Erie Canal ceased operations in 1913.

By the mid-19th century, railroads began to have an impact on the northern section of the Cuyahoga Valley. The Cleveland & Pittsburgh Railroad began operations in 1852 and maintained an alignment that crossed Tinker's Creek along the eastern edge of the valley. In 1880, the Valley Railway bisected the Cuyahoga Valley, leaving in its wake depots and new communities. New depot communities such as Thornburg and South Park emerged from the new railroad connection, while established communities such as Independence and Brecksville also built stops along the line. Heavily dependent on industrial commerce, the Valley Railway business connections brought new industrial developments to the valley in the early 20th century. Companies such as the Hydraulic Press Brick Company at South Park were dependent on their connection to the railroad for receiving raw resources and shipping finished products.

Jaite Paper Mill was also reliant on a railroad connection to do business. Founded by Charles Jaite in 1905, the Jaite Paper Mill manufactured bags for bulk-product industries such as flour and ready-mix cement. Jaite built his mill on the east side of the Cuyahoga River on a 22-acre site in Northfield Township (Summit County) along the banks of the Ohio & Erie Canal. However, the mill's operation did not utilize the canal as a transportation resource, but as a source of water for fire suppression. To facilitate a railroad connection, the Baltimore & Ohio Railroad built a siding and trestle over the river to connect to the mill. The railroad was used to move all products into and out of the site.

To house his mill's managers and workers, Jaite built a company town complete with nine company houses in Brecksville Township. These dwellings along with the company store/post office and railroad depots formed the core of "Jaite."

At its zenith, as many as 250 workers, many who were recent Polish immigrants, were employed at Jaite Paper Mill, producing up to eight tons of paper daily. One key to the mill's success was an abundant supply of fresh water provided by an artesian well on site. At peak operation, the mill pumped approximately 400,000 gallons of water each day from the well. The mill continued to produce paper until 1984. In the 1980s, the National Park Service purchased the company town. The rehabilitated buildings now serve as headquarters for Cuyahoga Valley National Park.

This photograph shows Alexander Mill and Lock 37 in 1898. (CVNP)

Numerous businesses sprang up along the banks of the Ohio & Erie Canal after its opening in 1827. Near the intersection of Rockside Road and the canal, John Zimmerman opened a tavern in 1830. Serving boat captains, canalers, and quarry men, the establishment earned a reputation as a rough-and-tumble place. By the late 19th century, the area around Zimmerman's became collectively known as "Thornburg." (*CVNP*)

Although not an original stop in 1880, the Cleveland Terminal & Valley Railroad added a standard combination station called South Park near the Village of Independence after taking over the Valley Railway in the late 19th century. This area contained a hydraulic brick press factory and company houses, which can be seen in the background of this photograph of the Flood of 1913. (*CVNP*)

This photograph shows State Boat #1 navigating the Ohio & Erie Canal south of Stone Road in 1902. The State of Ohio maintained "state boats," which were work crafts responsible for repairs and maintenance of the canal. State boats were assigned to specific sections of the canal, and the captains were usually locals. This view appears to be of a weekend pleasure trip. (*CVNP*)

In 1864, the Cleveland & Pittsburgh Railroad completed this cut-stone viaduct over Tinker's Creek Gorge, replacing an earlier wooden trestle. The viaduct, measuring 225 feet long and rising 120 feet above Tinker's Creek, took nearly three years to construct. This 1864 photograph captures the inaugural train ride over the new viaduct. (*BHS*)

Between 1901 and 1902, the Pennsylvania Railroad began a massive earth-moving project to facilitate a realignment of the tracks crossing Tinker's Creek where the stone viaduct stood. As a result, this section of the creek valley was filled in to create an earthen embankment. To allow Tinker's Creek to flow through the new embankment, a 512-foot sandstone block tunnel, known as the "Arch," was constructed. (*BHS*)

Between 1909 and 1911, the New York Central Railroad constructed a steel railroad trestle over Tinker's Creek. This photograph shows a track crane placing a girder during construction of the trestle. Operating mainly as a freight line, the New York Central Railroad hauled raw resources such as coal and stone through the valley for roughly five decades. (*CVNP*)

The New York Central Railroad operated in the valley until the service was abandoned in the late 1960s. The New York Central Railroad demolished the Tinker's Creek trestle in 1973. The railroad's right-of-way was sold to the Cleveland Electric Illuminating Company. The trestle site is now part of the Cleveland Metroparks' Bedford Reservation. (CVNP)

The house west of Lock 38 experienced several alterations over time. Constructed in the 1820s, the building served numerous functions during its history including a saloon, inn, dance hall, and general store. By the 1930s, the south section of the house was converted into a duplex with a two-story porch. In the late 1980s, the National Park Service rehabilitated the building into a visitor center and reintroduced its 19th century appearance. (CVNP)

16

Twelve-Mile Lock on the Ohio Canal.

Stereoview cards became fashionable in the late 19th century, especially views of "American Scenery." A stereoscopic viewer was used to provide a three-dimensional image of the photograph. Victorians would relax in their parlors with a box full of stereos and a viewer and be transported around the country and the world. This c. 1870s view of the Lock 38 area is one of the earlier photographs of the site. (CVNP)

Mr. and Mrs. Gorris posed for this 1890s photograph in front of their house, which later became Canal Visitor Center. Gorris worked as a blacksmith and most likely maintained his smithy north of his house along the Ohio & Erie Canal. (*CVNP*)

Built in 1836 by William Knapp, this house sits along Canal Road directly across from Lock 38. Knapp worked as a civil engineer and held numerous public offices including township clerk, tax assessor, postmaster, and Cuyahoga County surveyor. Into the 20th century, the property functioned as a farm with the Stephan Family maintaining a vegetable stand. Notice the two greenhouses on the right side of this 1930s photograph. (*CVNP*)

Historically, Riverview Road connected to Canal Road north of Tinker's Creek. During the early 20th century, an arch truss bridge carried Riverview Road over the Cuyahoga River. This 1902 photograph is of William Fish crossing the bridge in his new White Steamer. (*CVNP*)

The 19th century saw several grist mills operating in the Cuyahoga Valley. This *c.* 1915 view is of Alexander's Mill along the Ohio & Erie Canal south of Fitzwater Road. The mill was built in 1855 and originally contained a waterwheel, probably an undershot, powered by diverted water from the canal. In 1900, the mill was purchased by the Wilson family who remain the owners today. (*CVNP*)

By the 1920s, Alexander's Mill (renamed Wilson's Mill) had transformed from grist to feed milling as a result of changing consumer demands. This 1951 view is of miller Tom Wilson working in the mill. The Wilsons continued to use water power to drive their turbine until the 1970s. The mill no longer grinds grain but still operates as a feed and seed store. (CVNP)

This 1895 view of Lock 37 is taken from a northbound canal boat approaching the lock at Alexander's Mill (not captured in this photograph). The buildings in the left frame are a grocery store and saloon owned by V. Vanoucek. Notice the small rowboat near the floodgate and the mule skinner and team walking north. (*CVNP*)

In 1826, Stephen Frazee built his house along the east side of Canal Road in Independence Township. The Federal-style house is one of the oldest surviving structures in the Cuyahoga Valley. Frazee farmed the fields west of the Ohio & Erie Canal directly across from his brick farmhouse on Canal Road. The fields north of this house were used as pasture lands. (*CVNP*)

B.&O.R.R. Near Brecksville, Ohio.
Track turned over during Flood Mar. 25, 1913

The Flood of 1913 had a devastating effect on the infrastructure of the Baltimore & Ohio Railroad. The section north of the Brecksville Station was especially hard hit by flooding. This 1913 view illustrates the power of the flood waters, which left twisted tracks in their wake. (*CVNP*)

Brecksville was the location of a low-level dam and "feeder" that provided water for the Ohio & Erie Canal from the Cuyahoga River. This 1907 photograph, facing south, depicts the Cuyahoga River (*right*) paralleling the feeder channel (*center*) and the canal channel (*left*). Taken during the state's canal reconstruction efforts, a dredge boat can be seen in the foreground. (*CVNP*)

A group from a German Sunday school takes a canal boat tour and picnic in the Cuyahoga Valley and poses for this photograph at 17-Mile Lock (Lock 36) in the Pinery Narrows in 1886. By the late 19th century, the function of the Ohio & Erie Canal shifted to recreational day use, and the valley began to be appreciated for its scenic beauty and recreational resources. (CVNP)

In early 1930, Alfred M. Felgate, Cuyahoga County Bridge Engineer, designed the Brecksville/Northfield High-Level Bridge that carries State Route 82 over the Cuyahoga Valley at the Pinery Narrows at a height of 145 feet above the valley floor. Between 1930 and 1931, the Highway Construction Company built the bridge out of steel-reinforced concrete. The construction project provided jobs for locals during the beginning of the Great Depression. (Jet Lowe, HAER)

Daytrips to the valley were common. In this 1931 photograph, Lewis Willey of Ghent, Ohio and friend are enjoying an afternoon in the valley. They are parked on the Ohio & Erie Canal Towpath. The Brecksville Feeder is in the foreground, and the construction scaffolding for the Northfield/Brecksville High-Level Bridge is in the background. (*Gerald Wuchter*)

Built as an original stop on the Valley Railway in 1880, the Brecksville Station represented the interface between commerce and transportation in the Brecksville area. This early 20th century photograph, taken from Station Road, illustrates typical activity at the depot. A load of logs appears to be readied for shipment. Several structures located in the vicinity of the Brecksville Station are evident in the background. (*CVNP*)

Built in 1881 by the Massillon Bridge Company, Station Road Bridge is the oldest wrought iron truss bridge in the Cuyahoga Valley. After the opening of the Valley Railway, the Brecksville Station became an important transportation node. The Station Road Bridge served as the primary connection over the Cuyahoga River between Northfield and Brecksville. Consequently, Cuyahoga and Summit Counties split the $3,642 cost of the bridge. (*Jet Lowe, HAER*)

Prior to the construction of Jaite, the area that would become the town was part of Richard Vaughan's Farm. The Vaughan's Farmhouse was located north of present-day Vaughn Road east of the railroad tracks. Agricultural fields stretch south of the road. Note in this 1918 view the railroad's passenger depot. (*CVNP*)

In the early 20th century, the Cleveland Terminal & Valley Railroad added a stop at Jaite, then known as Vaughn Station. The stop was named after the Vaughans whose property was bisected by the line. Eventually, the railroad changed the station's name to Jaite. The smaller, hipped-roof building was the freight depot, and the other building served as the passenger station and "order shed." (*CVNP*)

(*above*) In 1924 at the corner of
Vaughn and Riverview Roads, the
Jaite Company built a store and post
office. During company ownership,
eighty workers slept in shifts in this
building. Over time, the building has
been utilized as a gas station, restaurant,
and church. In the 1980s, the National
Park Service purchased the company
town. The rehabilitated store now serves
as headquarters for Cuyahoga Valley
National Park. (*Kathleen Schnell*)

(*right*) Mary Gilbert served as the "post
mistress" for Jaite from approximately
1934 to 1945. Mary and her husband
William lived on the second floor
of the store. The Jaite Post Office
occupied a corner of the company store
and consisted of a desk, a stand of small
mailbox pigeonholes, and a back shelf.
Mary would send and receive mail
via the Baltimore & Ohio Railroad.
(*Kathleen Schnell*)

27

In 1905, Charles H. Jaite and Robert H. Jaite began construction on their paper mill sited between the Cuyahoga River and the Ohio & Erie Canal. Nearly 250 workers were employed at Jaite. Some lived in the company town; others resided in Peninsula and Boston, "commuting" to work on the towpath. In 1951, National Container Corporation purchased the mill from the Jaite family, ending the local ownership. (*CVNP*)

Jaite Paper Mill had a daily capacity of eight tons of manufactured paper that was made into flour and cement bags and sold directly to manufacturers of these products. The Jaite Mill later made fertilizer bags and bread sacks. This early photograph of the Jaite Bag Room indicates there was an elaborate maze of overhead line shafts, countershafts, leather belts, belt shifters, and pulleys that ran the shop's machinery. (*PLHS*)

In this photograph, Nettie Keller poses in the Jaite Paper Mill's "Box Room." The 1918 *Directory of Ohio Manufacturers* indicates that the Jaite Mill employed 214 workers, about one-third being women. Women worked both in the mill's front office and on the shop floor, primarily stitching bag seams. (*PLHS*)

The Jaite Paper Mill fostered a familial culture among their workers. The company printed a newsletter that contained information and updates about employees and their families. At lunch, workers pitched horseshoes in the center yard of the 22-acre mill site. Notice the rolls of paper stock that surround the horseshoe pit. (*PLHS*)

A group of Jaite Paper Mill workers pose for this photograph during a horseshoe match in 1960. Pictured from left to right are "Shorty" Movens, Bob Pollard, unidentified, Ben Lahoski, Barney Lahoski, and William Bray. (*PLHS*)

For the latter half of the 19th century, Jonas Coonrad operated a cheese factory on his Riverview Road farm. The Coonrad farmhouse and summer kitchen are caught in the background of this 1910 photograph. Jonas is seated in the chair, and the baby is his grandson Clayton Stanford. The women are unidentified. The farmhouse was rehabilitated by Cuyahoga Valley National Park and is utilized as a ranger station. (*CVNP*)

Two

Traveling from Brandywine to Boston

In 1805, James Stanford and Alfred Wolcott arrived in the Connecticut Western Reserve to survey lands that had belonged to Simon Perkins. They would become the first two settlers in 1806. Soon, other settlers arrived, and Boston Township was officially organized in 1811.

The arriving New Englanders chose Boston for its potential waterpower. Before construction of the Ohio & Erie Canal, the only known industry was located at Brandywine Falls, a few miles east of Boston. In 1814, George Wallace erected a sawmill and gristmill. In 1816, he added a distillery, which processed twelve bushels of grain per day and turned out 30 to 40 gallons of superb whiskey. Used as an article of barter, the whiskey became known as "Brandywine Currency." In 1820, a post office and woolen mill were added. By the 1830s, Brandywine had grown into a village that rivaled Cleveland in industry.

Two features of the Ohio & Erie Canal encouraged the rise of commerce in Boston. The first was the location of Lock 32. Between 1828 and 1836, a warehouse, two general stores, hotel, blacksmith shop, and broom factory were constructed near the lock. In 1835, the Boston Land and Manufacturing Company Store was built by Irad and Thomas Kelly, brothers of canal commissioner Alfred Kelly. Next door, Jim and Lucy Brown opened a tavern. Jim Brown became Boston's most notorious and colorful resident. Although he was a known counterfeiter, he was elected Justice of the Peace for Boston in 1834.

The second feature that aided the growth of commerce was Stumpy Basin. Located a few miles south, this marshy area flooded during the construction of the canal and created a large, wide basin. This basin provided an excellent location to turn canal boats and unload freight. During winter months, it served as a place to store canal boats and to harvest ice.

During the mid-19th century, the boat building industry thrived in Boston. It has been said that the villages of Boston and Peninsula monopolized the canal boat building trade in the state of Ohio. William Barnhart and James Fayerweather co-owned Boston's largest boat yard.

Mills were built to capitalize on the strong waterpower at the river dam in the early 1820s. The first mills were constructed on the east side of the Cuyahoga River in 1821 by Watrous Mather, who built a sawmill, and Talmon Bronson, who erected a gristmill. By 1890, the profitability of these small mills diminished, and they ceased operation.

In 1892, Samuel C. Dyke of Akron's American Marble and Toy Manufacturing Company re-tooled the flourmill and began to produce the first stone marbles in the United States. In 1899, the Akron Bag Company opened a 55-acre site on the western side of the river dam.

Between 1900 and 1923, Boston experienced its greatest period of growth. It became a company town. In 1902, the Akron Bag Company was incorporated as the Cleveland-Akron Bag Company. At its height, the mill employed nearly two hundred people, many of whom were Polish immigrants from Cleveland. The mill manufactured flour sacks and roofing paper. The company built six employee houses on Main Street and two duplex houses on Riverview Road. In 1905, a general store was constructed just south of the plant on the west bank of the river. The mill's effect on Boston was so overwhelming that the Valley Railway changed the name on the depot from "Boston" to "Boston Mill." In 1923, the bag company closed, and its workers found employment at the Jaite Paper Mill located a few miles north. The Cleveland-Akron Bag Company facility was acquired by the Union Trust Company in 1928 and then sold at a sheriff's auction to the Cleveland and Boston Company. In 1932 the mill was torn down.

The great Flood of 1913 devastated Boston. Half of the covered bridge over the river dam was destroyed. Four employee houses that were owned by the Cleveland-Akron Bag Company were swept into the river. Over one hundred people were homeless. Food and supplies ran short, but the Cleveland-Akron Bag Company aided the needy with provisions and supplies, bringing them in by wagon. In an attempt to lower the water level, 200 pounds of dynamite were discharged at the northeast corner of the dam. The blast dropped the water level by ten inches, relieving some of the flooding. The railroad tracks in and around Boston were completely washed away, and it was three months before service was restored.

Today, the mills, river dam, and covered bridge have disappeared. Visitors to the restored Ohio & Erie Canal Towpath Trail can stop by the restored 1835 Boston Store, now a visitor center with exhibits interpreting canal boat building in the valley, or view changing art exhibitions by local artists at the M.D. Garage.

This photograph shows the village of Boston, Ohio, c. 1910. (*PLHS*)

(*above*) In 1814, George Wallace erected a sawmill and gristmill at Brandywine Falls. In 1816, Wallace added a distillery, which processed twelve bushels of grain per day and turned out 30 to 40 gallons of superb whiskey. Used as an article of barter, the whiskey became known as "Brandywine Currency." Wallace shipped his goods on the Ohio & Erie Canal from Wallace Lock, Lock 33, named for the Wallace family. (*PLHS*)

(*right*) These falls powered the mills erected by George Wallace in 1814. In 1820, a post office and woolen mill were added. By the 1830s, Brandywine had grown into a village that rivaled Cleveland in industry. Today, Wallace House serves as a bed and breakfast, and many visitors come to enjoy the beauty of the falls. (*PLHS*)

James Stanford settled in Boston in 1806. James died in 1827, leaving the farm to his son George. George Stanford built this Greek Revival house in 1843. After George's passing in 1883, the home remained in family hands until the 1930s. In the late 1970s, the house was purchased by the National Park Service and is now operated by American Youth Hostels. (*PLHS*)

George Stanford was the son of James Stanford. He inherited his father's farm, and the farm was greatly improved by him. He served as Justice of the Peace for six years, and in 1833, he organized the Boston Moral Society, the forerunner to the Peninsula United Methodist Church. (*PLHS*)

GEO. STANFORD,
BOSTON TP.

MRS. G. STANFORD, DEC.
BOSTON TP.

Catherine Carter married George Stanford in 1828. The couple resided on the family farm in Boston and raised eight children. (*PLHS*)

35

This photograph shows Boston Mills Road facing west, *c.* 1900. Near the center of the photograph is the covered bridge that carried Boston Mills Road over the Cuyahoga River. Constructed in the mid-1800s, this bridge was badly damaged in the floods of 1898 and 1913. It was repaired both times. The covered bridge was demolished in 1926 and replaced by a modern bridge. (*PLHS*)

These Boston landmarks have sat side by side for a century. The house on the left was built in 1822 by Dr. Eleazer Mather and is listed with the Summit County Century Homes Association. The store on the right served as a place for religious gatherings, viewing motion pictures, a post office, and a general store. Boodey's Square Deal Food Store was located here from 1945 to 1970. (*PLHS*)

This is a photograph of Boston Lock, Lock 32. Between 1828 and 1836, a warehouse, two general stores, a hotel, blacksmith shop, and a broom factory were constructed near this lock. Soon after the canal opened through Boston in 1827, Jim Brown became the leader of a gang of notorious counterfeiters. (*PLHS*)

In 1832, Brown used counterfeit currency to buy merchandise in New Orleans to be resold in the Orient. He was caught and arrested and then acquitted. He returned to Boston and was promptly elected Justice of the Peace. However, he returned to his crooked ways and was arrested a second time. In 1865 he died from a fall on a canal boat. (*PLHS*)

Lucy Brown was the wife of Jim Brown. After Jim Brown was arrested the second time, she finally divorced him in 1851. Jim and Lucy's granddaughter, Laura, would later marry "Ohio's Match King" O.C. Barber. (*PLHS*)

A map from 1856 identifies this building as McBride's Grocery, located on the west side of Lock 32. In 1890, the grocery was owned by H. Monroe. An announcement from 1902 heralded the grand opening of the Davis Hotel at this location. While the new school was being built in 1908, space was leased here for classrooms. The post office was also located here at various times. (*PLHS*)

In 1835, the Boston Land and Manufacturing Company Store was built by Irad and Thomas Kelly, brothers of Canal Commissioner Alfred Kelly. Today, this store is a visitor center that interprets the craft of canal boat building. (*CVNP*)

This photograph shows Boston Mills Road facing east. Visible in the center of this image is the bridge that carried the road over the Ohio & Erie Canal. The first building on the right is the tavern owned by notorious counterfeiter, and Justice of the Peace, Jim Brown. Immediately beyond Brown's tavern is the Boston Land and Manufacturing Company building, now known as Boston Store Visitor's Center. (*PLHS*)

The first mills built on this location in Boston were constructed in 1821. In 1892, Samuel C. Dyke of Akron's American Marble and Toy Manufacturing Company re-tooled the old flour mill located at the east end of the Boston Mills Road Bridge. The mill manufactured the first stone marbles in the United States. The mill employed nearly 30 people and produced over 200,000 marbles a day. (*PLHS*)

The Cleveland-Akron Bag Company brought a new prosperity to the village of Boston. The company built six employee houses on Main Street, two duplexes on Riverview Road, and a general store on the west bank of the river. The mill employed nearly two hundred people manufacturing flour sacks and roofing paper. Many ethnic people migrated from Cleveland to work at the mill. (*PLHS*)

This is a photograph of workers at the Cleveland-Akron Bag Company on August 8, 1910. Pictured, from left to right, are Andrew Johnston (on horse), Will Stair (standing), Marcus ? (seated on log), ? Boros, John Johnston, Grover Johnston, Charles Evhart, and Amos Floder. (*PLHS*)

This is an interior photograph of the Cleveland-Akron Bag Company, c. 1910. These machines mixed pulp. The two gentlemen in the photograph are unidentified. The mill closed in 1923, and the facility was acquired by the Union Trust Company in 1928. The complex was torn down in 1932. (*PLHS*)

The Cleveland-Akron Bag Company built this company store just south of the plant on the west bank of the Cuyahoga River. The Boston General Store sold to workers on credit, but a motto on the sales receipts read "all bills must be paid in full every regular pay." Chester and Julia Zielenski managed this store for the bag company for years. The Zielenskis' purchased the building in 1925. (*PLHS*)

While the Cleveland-Akron Bag Company provided an economic boost to Boston, clean water was a necessity in paper manufacturing. A filter house was built along the river, but pollution from Akron soon made filtration impractical. This dam was built on Spring Creek behind the present day Boston Mill ski slopes in an effort to secure adequate water for the mill. (*PLHS*)

In 1869, Akron businessman David King secured a charter from the state legislature to construct the Akron & Canton Railway, which was incorporated in 1871 as the Valley Railway Company. The panic of 1873 delayed the completion of the railroad until 1880. On January 28, the first train left Cleveland and covered the 57 miles between Cleveland and Canton in two hours. Regular freight and passenger service began on February 2. (*PLHS*)

43

The Ohio & Erie Canal lost much of its passenger traffic due to the railroad. Along the rail route, stations were built at Botzum, Ira, Everett, Peninsula, Boston, and Jaite to handle passengers and freight. This photograph shows the station at Boston Mill, c. 1900. The two men are unidentified. (*PLHS*)

This photograph shows the railroad area at Boston Mill, c. 1910. It was taken from Zielenski Court facing southwest. (*PLHS*)

The village of Boston fared the worst among the Cuyahoga Valley communities hit by the great Flood of 1913. The covered bridge was partially destroyed. Four employee houses belonging to the Cleveland-Akron Bag Company were swept into the river. Over 100 people were homeless. Those who fled the rising waters were taken in by neighbors; some even stayed in the Boston schoolhouse. (*PLHS*)

The Flood of 1913 hit the company houses hard, washing four of them away. The house sinking on its foundation in this photograph was righted and is still standing. One of the lost houses can be seen on its side at the center of the photograph. (*PLHS*)

In an attempt to lower the water during the Flood of 1913, 200 pounds of dynamite were discharged at the northeast corner of the Boston Dam. The blast dropped the water level by ten inches, relieving some of the flooding. The rail tracks in and around Boston were washed away. It was three months before rail service was restored and residents received their mail, newspapers, and supplies. (*PLHS*)

In the mid-1840s, this schoolhouse was constructed from bricks manufactured at the Conger and Jackson brickyard. Located half way up Hines Hill Road on the left, the land was donated by canal boat builder James Fayerweather. When a new school was built down the hill, this building became the Christian Alliance Church. The "little red church on the hill" was demolished by the owner, Russell Jaite, in 1953. (*PLHS*)

In 1908, the Boston Township Board of Education financed the construction of a new school in Boston for $3500. This molded concrete block building would be used until the Boston Township High School was opened in 1930 in Peninsula. The school was used to shelter Boston residents during the Flood of 1913. The congregation from the Christian Alliance Church, now the Boston Community Church, bought the building in 1947 for $200. (*PLHS*)

Lonesome Lock, Lock 31, is a beautiful but dangerous lock. Horse and mule stealing, robberies, and murders reportedly took place here. The barn to the left, a house, and a sawmill operated by Sam Treat were the only structures that existed at this lock. Standing among the trees were several empty shanties built by the sawmill workmen. (*PLHS*)

This photograph shows a man washing his clothes at Lonesome Lock. (*CVNP*)

The schoolhouse in Union District #2 served students from both Boston and Northfield Townships. It was built overlooking Brandywine Falls in 1830 and was used until 1854. The schoolhouse, along with a farmhouse and four acres, was purchased by artist William Sommer in 1914 and served as his studio until his death in 1949. The building was torn down in 1969 to make way for I-271. (*PLHS*)

William Sommer (1867–1949) has been regarded as the "Cezanne of Ohio." Hired by the Works Progress Administration during the Depression, Sommer painted the murals in the Cleveland Public Library and made an indelible mark on the art of Northeast Ohio. His work is constantly being re-evaluated, and his stature rises year by year. (*PLHS*)

In 1923, the residents of Boston Township's northeast corner decided that they wanted to erect streetlights in their neighborhood. Needing the ability to sell municipal bonds to finance this effort, the area petitioned to be incorporated as the village of Boston Heights, and was officially created in February 1924. The Village Council voted in 1925 to purchase the former schoolhouse from the Township Board of Education for $500. (*PLHS*)

Chittenden's Corners is located at the intersection of Olde 8 Road and Route 303. Located here was a passenger platform for the interurban streetcar, a meat market, two taverns, a general store, a restaurant, and an amusement park. This building, which sat on the location of John's B.P., was John Fiedler's garage. Chittenden's Corners changed after the 1950s when improvements were made to Route 303 and Route 8. (*PLHS*)

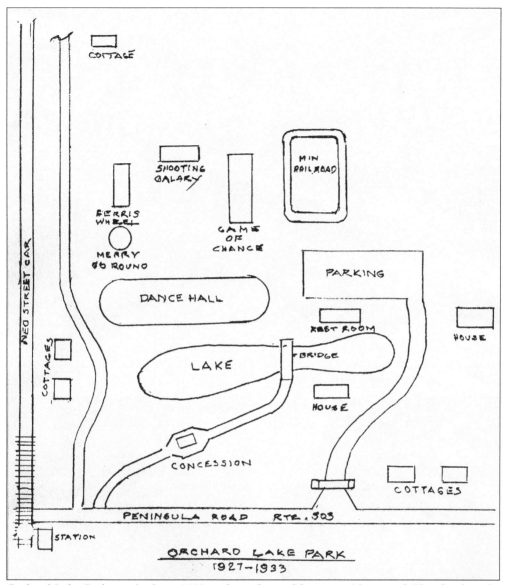

COTTAGE

SHOOTING GALARY

MIN RAILROAD

FERRIS WHEEL

GAME OF CHANCE

MERRY GO ROUND

NEO STREET CAR

PARKING

DANCE HALL

REST ROOM

HOUSE

COTTAGES

LAKE

BRIDGE

HOUSE

CONCESSION

COTTAGES

PENINSULA ROAD RTE. 303

STATION

ORCHARD LAKE PARK
1927–1933

Orchard Lake Park was built in 1927 and was located between Akron and Cleveland at the intersection of Route 8 and Route 303. Visitors came via the interurban streetcar, which followed the alignment of Route 8. Originally, plans were to build a roller coaster. Only a merry-go-round and Ferris wheel were installed. The dance hall was a great success. The park closed in 1933 due to the Great Depression. (*Dale Wagner*)

The Ohio Turnpike Commission was created by an act of the Ohio General Assembly in 1949. Groundbreaking ceremonies for the Ohio Turnpike were held October 27, 1952 on Riverview Road. This photograph was taken in 1954. (*PLHS*)

Sitting on twelve pairs of columns, the bridges were 2,682 feet long and carried the roadway 175 feet above the Cuyahoga River. The Ohio Turnpike, and Interstate 271 a decade later, brought the community closer to the outside world and all its traffic and commercial side effects. This photograph was taken in 1953 as the bridge under supports were being constructed. These bridges were replaced in 2003. (*PLHS*)

Three

A STOP IN
PENINSULA VILLAGE

Alonzo Dee was the first New Englander to settle in present-day Peninsula, in 1818. However, Hermon Bronson, who arrived in 1824, had the greatest effect on the village. It was Bronson who requested that the fledging village be surveyed in 1837 and officially christened it "Peninsula." Peninsula derived its name from a large bend in the Cuyahoga River that enclosed nearly 20 acres and looped within 50 feet of itself.

Peninsula grew due to its great potential for utilizing the available waterpower from a natural fall in the river. Hermon Bronson started the first sawmill and gristmill in Peninsula and was active in promoting Peninsula whenever possible, including the building of the Bethel Episcopal Church in 1839, which was renamed Bronson Memorial in 1889.

By 1825, Bronson campaigned to include Peninsula on the route of the proposed Ohio & Erie Canal. In 1827, the Ohio & Erie Canal opened in the valley, which included Lock 29 at Peninsula. More canal boats were built in the villages of Peninsula and Boston than in any other towns that were served by the canal. Jacob Barnhart was the pioneer of the boat building industry. He arrived in Peninsula in 1833 and established his yard south of Main Street. In 1839, Lawson Waterman settled in Peninsula and went into partnership with Jacob Barnhart. Eventually, Waterman owned the largest and best-known boatyard in the area.

The peak boat-building year was 1863 when 32 canal boats were built. The yards operated until the boat building industry diminished in the early 1870s and the yard workers found employment in the area's stone quarries.

For many years, one of the chief industries in the village was quarrying. When the construction of the Ohio & Erie Canal between Akron and Cleveland began in 1825, a ready supply of stone was found in the area now known as Deep Lock Quarry, and it was used in the building of the canal locks. After the use of its stone for the canal locks, Deep Lock Quarry manufactured grindstones, pulp stones, and millstones, which were shipped locally and also to Japan, Germany, and Russia. The quarry also supplied many stones used to construct foundations of many of the buildings in Peninsula. At one time, this quarry was owned by Ferdinand Schumacher who quarried millstones for use at his Quaker Oats Mill in Akron. The quarry continued its operation until 1917.

By 1870, Peninsula was a thriving community of 400 persons. There were two dry docks, and four boat yards. Canal boats plied up and down the canal loaded with freight, lumber, grain, coal, and sandstone. In addition, there were three blacksmith shops; a harness shop; three dry goods and grocery stores; three churches; a town hall that doubled as a theatre; and two hotels, the Seeley and the Cassidy, both with saloons. The Seeley was one of the largest and most famous hotels between Akron and Cleveland.

Even before the completion of the canal, there was talk of building railroads in Ohio. Just as Hermon Bronson campaigned to have the route of the Ohio & Erie Canal come through the village, his son Hiram V. Bronson negotiated with the Valley Railway to have the railroad line and a depot in Peninsula. In addition to a half-acre parcel to build a depot, Bronson conveyed to the railway company the ability to cut through the namesake "peninsula" and avoid the expense of building two bridges over the Cuyahoga River. Construction began on the Valley Railway in 1873 but was not completed until 1880. The railway not only brought goods but also introduced visitors from Akron and Cleveland to recreational opportunities in the valley.

The advent of the automobile had an effect on the populace. It now allowed the valley residents greater access to the cities of Cleveland and Akron. Furthermore, the city residents ventured frequently into the valley and began to settle here, thus beginning the area's suburban era. Another by-product of the automobile was an increase in recreational activities in the valley, which were heavily dependent on transportation to succeed.

Today, the village of Peninsula thrives; the community has worked to preserve a historic district that contains numerous public buildings and houses that are recognized by the National Register of Historic Places. The refurbished Ohio & Erie Canal Towpath is now a hike-and-bike trail along the Ohio & Erie Canalway and the Cuyahoga Valley Scenic Railroad makes regular stops in the village.

This is a photograph of the village of Peninsula from East Hill, *c*. 1880. (*PLHS*)

(*above*) The Bronsons built this impressive stone house on Main Street in 1845. The house still stands today opposite the Bethel Episcopal Church, which was renamed Bronson Memorial in 1889. (*PLHS*)

HERMON BRONSON,

BOSTON TP. O.

(*right*) Hermon Bronson moved to the area in 1824. He was the largest landowner and started the first sawmill and gristmill in Peninsula. Until his death in 1853, Hermon was active in promoting Peninsula whenever possible, including the building of the Bethel Episcopal Church in 1839. (*PLHS*)

Approaching the center of town is the Main Street Bridge. It had the reputation of being the toughest spot in Ohio. A saloon was located at each end of the bridge. It took longer to cross

This stereo card shows the Main Street Bridge facing east as it crossed both the Ohio & Erie Canal and the Cuyahoga River. The two-story building in the center of the bridge is Broughton's Saloon,

the canal here than at any other point due to the drinking and fighting among the boatmen who had spent time in the saloons. (*PLHS*)

which sat on a narrow strip of land between the two bodies of water. The saloon was accessible from both the bridge and the canal towpath. The building to the right is Cole's Store. (*PLHS*)

57

In 1839, Lawson Waterman settled in Peninsula and went into partnership with Jacob Barnhart, a pioneer of the boat building industry. Eventually, Waterman owned the largest and best-known boatyard in the area. He amassed a modest but honest fortune. In 1850, he purchased acreage and built a farmhouse. Today the home and farm is known as Heritage Tree Farms and is still owned by Waterman's descendants. (*PLHS*)

Waterman owned the largest and best-known boatyard in the area. His yard had a large amount of frontage on the canal, accommodating the construction of four boats at a time. The main building consisted of two stories. The first floor housed his carpenters and jointers. The second floor contained the painters' shop and an office. The yard operated until the boat building industry died out in the early 1870s. (*PLHS*)

While John Conger and Erastus Jackson opened the first brickyard in Boston in 1844, it was the Bronson family who would make the industry profitable. This advertisement is for the Bronson Brickworks, *c.* 1875. (*PLHS*)

The Bronson family opened a large brickyard along the canal just north of the aqueduct over the Cuyahoga River. Clay was dug from the steep hillside above the canal, put through a milling process to pulverize the clumps, mixed with water, molded into bricks, and then fired. The company employed 12 men who manufactured 15,000 bricks per day. (*PLHS*)

This building was erected in 1857 by Boston Township for use as a town hall and schoolhouse. After the village was incorporated in 1859, with Hiram V. Bronson as the first mayor, the village held its meetings here. This building was sold by the Board of Education to the village of Peninsula for $1.00 in 1939. Today, it houses the police station for the village. (*PLHS*)

In order to build the depot, Hiram V. Bronson conveyed to the Valley Railway Company the ability to cut through the namesake "peninsula" and avoid the expense of building two bridges over the Cuyahoga River. The catch in the agreement stated that "all passenger trains passing along the railway shall stop for a reasonable time to receive and discharge passengers." (*PLHS*)

Construction began on the Valley Railway in 1873 but was not completed until 1880. Just as Hermon Bronson campaigned to include Peninsula on the route of the canal, his son, Hiram V. Bronson, was negotiating with the Valley Railway to include Peninsula as a stop along the rail line. Hiram gave the rail company a half-acre parcel to build a depot in Peninsula. (*PLHS*)

Hermon Bronson first channeled through the narrow piece of land that formed the village's peninsula in 1832. At this location, he built a gristmill, which operated successfully for 70 years. The site was sold several times before it was bought by George and Oscar Thomas. In 1882, they remodeled the mill and earned the honor of owning the first mill in Northern Ohio to adopt the roller method. (*PLHS*)

In 1879, George Thomas' son entered into business with Chandler Moody of Cleveland. Their firm, Moody and Thomas, purchased the Peninsula mill in 1902. The mill produced "Household Favorite" and "Peerless Patent" flours. After the railroad came through town, a bridge was built over the Cuyahoga River to connect to the mill. The Moody and Thomas mill mysteriously burned to the ground on December 26, 1931. (*PLHS*)

Leander Beers, a blacksmith, arrived in Peninsula in 1849. In 1885, he built this structure next to his blacksmith shop and opened a general store. In 1915, it was sold to the Harrington family who operated the store and a post office until 1966. Today, this building houses the Yellow Creek Trading Company. (*PLHS*)

Built *c.* 1820, this building was the first permanent structure in Peninsula. In 1863, Frederick Wood bought the building and opened a store under the name of Fred Wood and Son. This store sold dry goods, groceries, drugs, and medicines until the turn of the century. Today, this building houses the Crooked River Herb Farm Shop. (*PLHS*)

Peninsula had four stone quarries that would eventually be controlled by the Cleveland Stone Company. At one time, this quarry, known as "Deep Lock" Quarry, was owned by Ferdinand Schumacher and produced millstones for his Quaker Oats Mill in Akron. Stones were used locally in Akron and Cleveland, but they also were shipped overseas to Japan, Germany, and Russia. (*PLHS*)

To facilitate shipment by water, a dock with a turning mill along with a 40-foot derrick for hoisting the stone aboard canal boats was constructed near Lock 28. The derrick can be seen toward the center of this photograph. The turning mill was the location where the stones were fashioned into grindstones, pulp stones, and millstones and stacked ready for shipment. (*PLHS*)

In the mid-1880s, Henry Currier leased land for this quarry from Mrs. Lawson Waterman. Eventually, this lease was sold to the Independent Stone Company and later to the Cleveland Stone Company. A narrow gauge railroad connected Currier's quarry to the Valley Railway at Deep Lock Quarry. This quarry ceased operation in 1920. It eventually filled with water from a natural spring, and is now a popular swimming hole. (*PLHS*)

The Main Street Bridge consisted of two spans: one over the Cuyahoga River and one over the Ohio & Erie Canal. The span over the canal was completely destroyed by the Flood of 1913, leaving the village divided by water. Broughton's Saloon at the right was vacated during the flood, but it eventually fell into the river. (*PLHS*)

The Flood of 1913 completely destroyed the Ohio & Erie Canal. It washed away Lock 29 at Peninsula and the aqueduct. (*PLHS*)

The tracks at the Peninsula Depot were rendered unusable for many weeks. The Mill Street Bridge, which originated just beyond the small tree in the center of this photo, was completely washed away. (*PLHS*)

As the floodwaters receded, the damage to the railroad was enormous. (*PLHS*)

After the arrival of the Valley Railway, Andrew Cassidy and Samuel McNeil capitalized on the local cheese market. Even J.B. Stouffer of Richfield, whose family would go on to found the enormous Stouffer Foods Corporation, sold his Peninsula factory to Cassidy and McNeil. The partners had 13 "depots" where cheese could partially solidify before being moved to this main factory/warehouse in Peninsula. (*PLHS*)

The Peninsula Banking Company opened to much fanfare in January 1911 and weathered the teens and twenties. The Great Depression hit the institution hard, forcing the bank to close its doors in March 1933 for one of Roosevelt's "banking holidays." Although the Peninsula Banking Company never re-opened, its depositors were paid in full by 1937. (*PLHS*)

This building was constructed in 1851 and served as a one-room schoolhouse for Boston Township's Sub-district #6 until 1887 when a new school was built across Riverview Road. Through an act of the Ohio State Legislature in 1888, the village spent $500 to remodel the hall to befit the activities of the G.A.R. (Grand Army of the Republic), a fraternal organization of Civil War Veterans. (*PLHS*)

The Peninsula G.A.R. Post was named in memory of George Waterman, the eldest son of Lawson and Angeline Waterman. George served in Company E, First Regiment, and Ohio Volunteer Infantry. He received an army commission from Ohio Governor David Tod to the 155th Regiment O.V.I. stationed in Dayton. On September 2, 1863, the evening before his furlough, he was shot chasing southern sympathizers. He died on September 19. (*PLHS*)

Civil War veteran Arthur L. Conger and his wife, Emily Bronson, dedicated this monument to honor the 141 enlistees from Boston Township who served in the War of the Rebellion on July 4, 1889. Cannons were fired, many speeches were given, local girls paraded in white gowns while representing states of the union, and local and state dignitaries were celebrated.

The monument sat in the intersection of Route 303 and Riverview Road until 1932 when an automobile struck the statue and the head fell off. A ransom note was left that said the head would be returned when the statue was moved. The statue was permanently relocated to Cedar Grove Cemetery by Memorial Day of 1933, and the head was returned. (*PLHS*)

By 1917, the G.A.R. waned as the Civil War veterans aged. The hall was turned over to the village and was used as a dance school; meeting place for Grange, 4-H, and Boy Scouts; a movie theater, and a gymnasium for school basketball and volleyball games. From 1943 to 1949, the G.A.R. Hall was also the home of the Peninsula Players, a group of amateur thespians. (*PLHS*)

The American Legion played a vital role in the life of the community and organized Memorial Day parades that continue to this day. In 1921, the returning WWI veterans organized the American Legion post and were given the use of the G.A. R. Hall. By the end of the 1950s, the American Legion post had become inactive, and the hall reverted to the State of Ohio American Legion. (*PLHS*)

The stick-style Peninsula High School building was constructed in 1887 and had a bell tower with a slate roof. A brick addition was built in 1919. When a new high school was constructed in 1930, the old school was sold to the Trustees of Boston Township. The Union Grange #2380 met in the wood building, and the Boston Township Trustees met in the brick building. (*PLHS*)

The class of 1929 was the last to graduate from Peninsula High School at Route 303 and Riverview Road. Upon returning from the holidays in January 1930, each student carried their belongings to the new Boston Township High School on Bronson Avenue. The Boston Township Schools annexed the Northampton Township Schools in 1958 to create Woodridge Local Schools. This building is currently known as Woodridge Intermediate School. (*PLHS*)

73

Every high school boy was drafted to complete the 1923 Peninsula High School football team shown in this practice session. In the background are the original Bigelow Chevrolet buildings and the Boston Township Soldiers' Monument. Pictured, from left to right, are: (front row) Jimmy Genovese, Girden Harrington, Larry Truxell, Ray Hall, Francis Stebbins, Richard Sweitzer, and Robert Conger; (back row) Garnet Moore, Jim Kennedy, Clayton Stanford, Ernie Genovese, and Henry Herr (Principal). (*PLHS*)

The Peninsula High School girls' basketball team from 1924 consisted of nine players. Since the school building had no gymnasium, games were played half-court style across the street at the G.A.R. Hall. Pictured, from left to right, are: (front row) Agnes Gillette, Nellie Point, Marion Wise, Emily Kennedy, and Bertha Rodatt; (back row) Katheryn Conger, Henry Herr (Principal), Josephine Mayer, Mary Rockwood, Lucille Ritch, and unidentified. (*PLHS*)

During the winter, Old Thunderbolt was the super-bobsled in the village. It was factory made, store bought, and professionally painted in bright yellow with red trim. Store Hill in the center of the village was the popular place for coasting. The coasters are, from left to right, Scotty Ingerton, Frank McNab, Ben Gillette, Coonie Smith, Bert Stebbins, Frank (Buster) Chamberlin as steersman, and Buster's white dog. (*PLHS*)

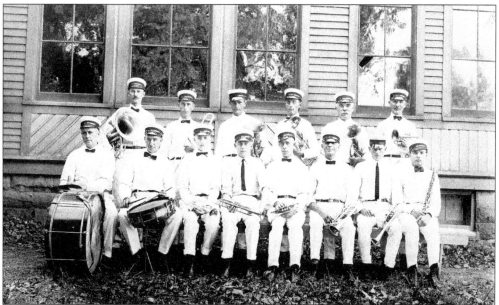

The Peninsula band performed on a bandstand, which formerly sat in front of the Village Hall. The band performed for celebrations and special occasions. In this *c.* 1915 photograph, from left to right, are: (front row) Harvey Bean, Dan Billings, Wallace Payn, Jules Boodey, Ashell Currier, George Boodey, Ed Ely, and Al Keller; (back row) Mac Payn, Grover Morris, Fred Rodatt, Alva Morris, Ed Currier, and Nelson Mackey. (*PLHS*)

In 1835, Hermon Bronson organized a Protestant Episcopal Church. It was dedicated in 1839 as "Bethel Episcopal Church." In 1889, the church was remodeled by Bronson's daughter-in-law, Mrs. Ruth Ranney Bronson, and renamed "Bronson Memorial Church." The Episcopal community dwindled, and in 1955, services were discontinued. The property was transferred from the Episcopal Diocese of Ohio to the Summit County Historical Society in 1965. (*PLHS*)

Located on the east side of the village is the Peninsula United Methodist Church, built in 1869. The first Methodist organization, the Boston Moral Society, was organized in 1833 by George Stanford of Boston. Its goals were "regulation of the Burying Ground" and the holding of "Religious Meetings on the Sabbath." These "religious meetings" resulted in the appearance of circuit rider preachers and finally the construction of this church. (*PLHS*)

Mother of Sorrows Catholic Church was built in 1882. The first recorded Catholic activity in the Peninsula area was in 1825 during the construction of the canal since many workers were Irish Catholic. New industries brought an influx of Polish, Slovenian, and Italian immigrants to the area. By 1928, two-thirds of the membership at Mother of Sorrows was Polish. In 1935, the church was enlarged. (*PLHS*)

Now the location of the Fisher's Restaurant parking lot, this hotel was built in the mid-1800s by Stephen Edgerly. Andrew Cassidy, a local cheese maker, purchased the hotel in 1878. Over the years, the building housed restaurants, confectionaries, appliance stores, barbershops, and boarding rooms. It was demolished in 1961. Behind this building, motion pictures were shown in an outdoor theatre. Unfortunately, passing trains caused many unplanned intermissions. (*PLHS*)

Three Peninsula landmarks of the 1950s line the north side of Route 303. Scotty's Place at the far left was owned by former professional baseball player Scotty Ingerton. The building to the right was the Peninsula Nite Club. The building in the center was built by Merrill Boody around 1860 as a general store. At that time, the downstairs served at a general store and the upstairs an opera house. (*PLHS*)

German immigrant Anton Pfaus arrived in Peninsula in 1867 and engaged in the shoemaking business. Pfaus built a little false-front building on the southwest corner of Main and Locust Streets in 1888. In 1914, Pfaus sold the property to George Bergdorf who ran the store as a meat market until his son, Raymond, took over. Raymond ran the meat market until 1950. (*PLHS*)

The engine house of the Peninsula Fire Department in this 1940 photograph was remodeled into offices. In 1976, Peninsula and Boston Township formed the Valley Fire District. Pictured, from left to right, are: (front row) J.D. Morgan, Rollin Morgan, Forrest Boose, Raymond Bergdorf, George Fisher, and Charlie Wurzbacher; (back row) Del Ritch, Al Ritch, Sig Wojtkowski, Leonard Morris, Dick Billings, Ed Eberle, John Ritch, George Tellings, and Paul Groff. (*PLHS*)

During the golden age of radio, *Lum and Abner* premiered in 1931. The show was sponsored by the Quaker Oats Company located in Akron, Ohio. Because of this local connection, *Lum and Abner* made an appearance in Cleveland and Peninsula in 1933 for a publicity shoot. A fake sign was hung at the present-day Downtown Emporium representing the fictional Jot-em-Down Store in the fictional town of Pine Ridge, Arkansas. (*PLHS*)

During the 1930s, John Ozmun owned a Plymouth agency and garage three doors east of the present-day Winking Lizard. In this photograph, he is sitting in his 1900 Holsman, a one-cylinder automobile operated with a tiller instead of a steering wheel. In 1939, Ozmun drove this car from San Diego to the New York World's Fair. He sold ten-cent postcards of his automobile to finance his trip. (*PLHS*)

Since 1960, this building has housed Fisher's Resturant. Prior to the restaurant, the building served as a funeral parlor, Billings' Ford Agency, Conger's Store, and Wells' Store. At the time of this 1923 photograph, Dan Billings, standing in the door, had a showroom in the front and repair bays in the rear. In the 1980s, the original structure was renovated, and the gas pumps were removed. (*PLHS*)

In 1911, Bigelow Motors opened on the southeast corner of Route 303 and Riverview Road. Owner Herb Bigelow switched from Studebakers to Chevrolets in 1914. The original building burned in 1928, and a Spanish-style, stucco building was built on the site. This 1948 photograph shows Doug Bigelow, Dick Bigelow, and Bob Conger looking at a car to be raffled off. In 1972, Bigelow Chevrolet moved to Parma, Ohio. (*PLHS*)

In 1947, the Peninsula Library moved into the Boston Township Hall and stayed there until 1964. Always eager to increase the collections, the library acquired the holdings of Edwin Shaw Hospital in 1954. Local resident Clair Mantz (in the baseball cap) was president of the Norka Beverage Company and volunteered his company's truck to move the collection, aided by many local citizens. Norka is, of course, Akron spelled backward. (*PLHS*)

In 1942, Peninsula Girl Scout leaders Ruth Roush and Frena Wilcox were looking for a project to sponsor. Local artist Honore' Cooke suggested they start a library. A Halloween party requiring the donation of a book for admission was held, and a library opened in the Peninsula Village Hall in 1943. In 1964, Robert Bordner secured funds to build a new structure on Riverview Road. (*PLHS*)

After 1900, most communities had baseball teams and playing fields. One Peninsula player, Scotty Ingerton, later played professionally with the Boston Nationals. The players are pictured, from left to right, as follows: (front row) Frank Stebbins, Herm Pfaus, and Bert Stebbins; (middle row) Tommy Wynne, Scotty Ingerton, and Fred Bishop; (back row) Ralph Bowers, Earl Seeley, Bill Lamma, Alton Keller, Jim Morris (umpire), Charley Bishop (manager), Charles Currier (scorekeeper), Julian Morgan, Neil Ingerton, and Leo Stebbins. (*PLHS*)

From the 1930s through the 1960s, Peninsula was the location of a convergence of motorcyclists during the summer months. Using the back side of the "Pinnacle," the Greater Akron Motorcycle Club sponsored a professional hill climb sanctioned by the American Motorcycle Association. The sea of motorcycles and spectators shown in this 1962 photograph are located on the current site of the Lock 29 Trailhead parking lot. (*PLHS*)

The Peninsula Players began in 1942 with *The Spooky Tavern* as their first production. Plays were performed in the Boston High gymnasium, in the historic G.A.R. Hall, and in the evenings in a circus tent on the Boston Township property. This photograph depicts the players in their 1953 production of *Angel in the Pawnshop*. (*PLHS*)

Local author Fred Kelly donated a few acres along Route 303 east of Peninsula to the Peninsula Players who, in 1953, remodeled a barn into a state-of-the-art theatre. Their production from the 1948 comic strip *Li'l Abner* was the first ballet ever televised. The Players' last production was in 1974. Today, the barn is known as the Players Barn antique shop. (*PLHS*)

Four

TRAVELING FROM EVERETT TO BOTZUM

Everett, Ira, and Botzum are three valley communities historically located south of Peninsula. Each evolved due to the construction of the Ohio & Erie Canal. With the arrival of the Valley Railway, however, the name of each of community was changed.

The village of Everett was originally named Johnnycake after an event that has become canal folklore. In 1828, a spring storm dumped mounds of sand and debris into the canal, bringing boats to a standstill. Until crews could dig out the canal, travelers were stranded at Lock 27, and supplies ran short. Cornmeal, the only staple in abundance, was turned into johnnycakes and fed to the travelers.

Henry Iddings was Everett's first settler before 1820, but he sold his property to Alanson Swan in 1827. Swan then opened the first tavern and store. By 1835, a post office opened and served the area until the 1950s. The community is home to a covered bridge that was constructed in 1876. Today, the Everett Road Covered Bridge is one of the most familiar and loved landmarks in the valley.

With the arrival of the Valley Railway in 1880, the depot was named Everett to honor Sylvester T. Everett, vice president and treasurer of the Valley Railway Company. With the naming of the depot, the surrounding community also became known as Everett.

Religious services had been held in Everett for decades. However, a church building was not constructed until 1901. Tragically, the building was destroyed by fire in 1908. The Everett Church of Christ was rebuilt on the same location in 1909. Presently, this church is still functioning and is known as The Church in the Valley.

Two miles south of Everett is the hamlet of Ira. In 1810, Jonathan Hale and Jason Hammond took possession of acreage purchased from the Connecticut Land Company and were Ira's first two settlers. Life at Ira also developed around the Ohio & Erie Canal and Lock 26, Pancake Lock. This lock also got its name during the same spring flood of 1828 that gave Johnnycake Lock its name. Flour was the only staple on the canal boats. It was made into pancakes and fed to the stranded passengers and boatmen.

Unlike Everett, there were no churches, stores, or taverns in Ira. It was a community of residences and farms. Samuel McNeil ran a cheese factory just north of Pancake Lock, and the farmers brought him their milk to process into cheese. Once the Valley Railway came through, farmers shipped milk into Akron to be processed by the Akron Pure Milk Company.

The depot near the community of Ira was named Hawkins for Ira Hawkins whose land was crossed by the tracks. Confusion with another stop named Haskins resulted in the name of the station being changed to Ira. From 1875 to 1924, the railroad not only brought goods but also summer boarders to stay at Hale's farm. The third generation of the family to live on the farm, C.O. Hale, grandson of the original Ira settler Jonathan Hale, invited paying guests who provided the economic base for his farm.

In 1883, Henry Willett Howe established a post office at Ira and became its first postmaster. In 1887, Henry's son Frank shared the space in the post office building and operated a small printing company, the F.R. Howe Printing Company. The post office officially closed in 1953.

Two miles south of Ira was the hamlet of Boztum, which was sometimes known as Buckeye or Niles. Botzum's development was also due to the Ohio & Erie Canal. The canal at Yellow Creek had no berm bank on the west, which created the Yellow Creek Basin. The basin was a good location for businesses to develop. In 1827, Nathanial Hardy established a hotel, two warehouses, and small store.

In 1836, 100 acres at the mouth of Yellow Creek were platted into a village and given the name of Niles. Due to the financial panic of 1837, investors never constructed this village. It remained a village only on paper, and its lots were sold off. One of the purchasers was John George Botzum.

A post office was established in 1866, and it operated under the name of Buckeye. However, the Valley Railway renamed the depot stop Botzum after the major landowner in this area. In 1893, the post office also changed its name to Botzum.

Today, the hamlet of Botzum no longer exists. In 1922, the Botzum brothers sold 800 acres to the City of Akron for construction of the Akron sewage disposal plant.

This is a photograph of Walnut Grove Farm owned by Frank Reifsnider. This photograph was taken at the eastern end of present-day Bolanz Road. The village of Everett is at the far right. (*PLHS*)

The Oak Hill School was typical of the many one-room schoolhouses in the area. Constructed in 1885 on the northwest corner of Oak Hill and Scobie Roads, the building was used until 1911 when the students transferred to the centralized school in Peninsula. An effort by neighbor Ruth Roush to move the school and restore it was not successful. The schoolhouse was demolished in 1966. (*PLHS*)

John H. Gilson was a native of England who moved to Ohio in 1841 and owned a 116-acre farm two miles south of Peninsula. On February 1, 1877, Mr. Gilson drowned accidentally in Furnace Run. His body was not recovered until four days later. Mrs. Gilson lived on the farm until her death. Their daughter Elizabeth married Hiram Lee. This photograph is the Gilson/Lee family at the Gilson homestead. (*PLHS*)

This is a photograph of Hazel Dell Farm on Oak Hill Road, *c.* 1925. Hector Ozmun, born on his parents Boston Township farm in 1815, moved to this property in the 1840s. In 1871, Hector became a partner in the Boston Union Cheese Factory. Ozmun's grandson, Albert Bell, was very prominent in the agricultural affairs of Summit County and lived on this farm until his death in 1973. (*PLHS*)

A number of influential and artistic families relocated to the Oak Hill area and were dubbed "Peninsula's Artist Colony." Pictured, from left to right, are: (front row) Ruth Roush, Honore-Guilbeau Cooke, Sally Roush, Julius Kubinyi, and Bob Bordner; (middle row) Jeremy Cooke, Galen Roush as Santa, Jennifer Cooke, Hamlin Sanford, Nancy Sanford, and Eleanora Buchla Kubinyi; (back row) Ben Coates, Buck Cooke, Peg Coates, Ruth King Bordner, Kay Moore, and Jim Roush. (*PLHS*)

Johnnycake Lock, Lock 27, is on the Ohio & Erie Canal. Canal folklore played in the naming of this lock. In 1828, a spring rainstorm dumped mounds of debris into the canal. It brought canal traffic to a standstill. For three days, passengers and boatmen were stranded at Alanson Swan's tavern. Cornmeal, the only staple in abundance, was made into Johnnycakes, which they ate morning, noon, and night. (*PLHS*)

Three miles south of Peninsula, nestled between the area known as Oak Hill and the banks of Furnace Run, is the village of Everett. It was served by both the Ohio & Erie Canal and the Valley Railway. Everett had a general store, post office, rail stop, schoolhouse, church, and covered bridge. The Western Union Telegraph and American Express Companies both did business here. (*PLHS*)

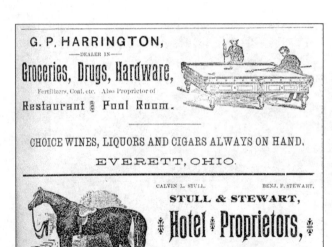

In 1885, Gurden P. Harrington, who operated the hotel, grocery store, post office, restaurant, and pool hall, took out an advertisement in the county business directory. Just below Harrington's advertisement, Calvin Stull and Benjamin Stewart placed one. They not only owned and ran a store but also provided a horse breeding and dealer business. (*PLHS*)

Although Everett had a small commercial community, it was surrounded by very hilly country. The bottomland along the Cuyahoga River was fertile, and farmers raised a variety of crops. However, the majority of farmers in this area were dairy farms. Farmers took their milk to the Everett depot and shipped it into Cleveland and Akron. This scene is along Everett Road opposite the church. (*PLHS*)

In 1931, "Big Jim" Szalay moved to the area and began growing sweet corn. He started out with 67 acres and quickly increased it to include 300 acres. Today, many visitors to the valley stop at Szalay's to buy sweet corn. (*PLHS*)

Taken in 1955, this photo shows Everett Road facing east. In the center of the photograph is the railroad crossing and Kepner's store. At the right are the fields owned by the Akron Metropolitan Park District for their tree nursery. At the far left is Hamilton's store. Next to Hamilton's store is the house where the family of "Big Jim" Szalay lived when they first moved to the valley. (*PLHS*)

After 1920, Frank Ivel Kepner built a store on the corner of Everett and Riverview Roads. Frank's parents, wanting a boy but getting a girl, conceded to her gender by reversing the letters in her middle name from "Levi" to "Ivel." Frank was Everett's postmistress from 1917 to 1948. She is standing in the doorway of the store. The store was burned down in 1969. (*PLHS*)

The general store at 2185 Everett Road was built by Gurden Harrington sometime before 1860. Maude Carter owned the store during the Great Depression, and it became a gathering place in Everett with on-going card games and a communal telephone. Behind the counter are Bruce and Bertie Hamilton, owners from 1944 to 1967. Bertie served as the postmistress from 1948 to 1953 when Everett's post office was closed. (*PLHS*)

Mail clerk Clara Sager from the Everett post office prepares to hang the mailbag. A hook on the mail car of the next train will snatch the mailbag without stopping. The mail car on the non-stop Akron-Cleveland train leaving the Akron station at 8:00 a.m. would catch all of the valley mail and have it sorted and ready for delivery at the Cleveland post office within one hour. (*PLHS*)

After the railroad, the next postal delivery in the valley, as well as the nation, was Rural Free Delivery (RFD). In 1896, Congress enacted RFD. Rural citizens no longer had to drive to the post office. Mail was delivered to their mailboxes outside their own front door. This photograph is postal deliveryman Clarence Vogel in his mail truck. (*PLHS*)

This is a photograph of the cleaning party after the construction of the church building for the United Brethren in Everett, Ohio, January 9, 1895. This congregation dissolved in 1899 and the building stood empty until 1901. Pictured, from left to right, are: (front row) Sarah Chamberlain, Maria Ferguson, Elwin Muar, Elva Muar, Elbridge Burritt, and ? Burritt; (back row) William Bower, Abbey Bower Lee, Susan Warner Bower, Eugene Muar, and Lina Carter. (*PLHS*)

In 1901, the Everett Church of Christ was organized and moved into the abandoned United Brethren building. Tragically, the building was destroyed by a fire in 1908. With the help of area churches, the church was rebuilt on the same location. In the 1990s the church was renamed The Church in the Valley. Today, it is an active and thriving church. (*PLHS*)

Everett Grange #1360 was in existence from 1890 to 1895. Union Grange #2380 was organized in Peninsula in 1924. Families in Everett, including the Broughtons, Bowlings, and Osbornes, had a major influence on the group's activities. This street dance was organized by the Union Grange in 1949 and was held at the intersection of Everett and Riverview Roads. These events contributed to the social life of the community. (*PLHS*)

The Everett Covered Bridge is one of the most familiar and loved landmarks in the Cuyahoga Valley, popular to artists, photographers, and history buffs. Through current research, the construction date of the bridge is 1876. During its history the bridge had been damaged a number of times. However in 1975, a severe storm destroyed it beyond repair. In 1986, it was reconstructed and opened to non-vehicular traffic. (*PLHS*)

This is a photograph of Pancake Lock, Lock 26 at Ira. The two-story frame house to the right of the photograph belonged to Charles and Susan Carter. Charles served as "lock tender." He also owned 56 acres on which he had a very prosperous dairy farm. (*PLHS*)

HAWKINS CHEESE FACTORY, *July* 1901

M *E F Craig*

By 3159 *lbs. Milk, at*....... *Cts. per Gallon,* $........... $ 25.21

By........... *lbs. Milk, at*........... *Cts. per Gallon,*

To........... *lbs.*...........*at*........... *Cts. per lb.,*

To........... *lbs.*...........*at*........... *Cts. per lb.,*

This receipt is from the cheese factory that was built in Ira. In addition to shipping their milk into Cleveland and Akron, the farmers sold their milk to the cheese factory, which contributed to the economy in Ira. Each month farmers received a check for the milk they delivered to the cheese factory. (*PLHS*)

The railroad provided many services to Ira residents and brought the city and county closer together. High school students found it easier to take the train into Akron to attend Akron Central High School than to struggle with the muddy roads to attend Bath High School. The train's faster schedule gave farmers in Ira the means to sell their milk to the dairies in the cities. (*PLHS*)

One of the first rail stations to be established along the Valley Railroad was Hawkins, named for Ira Hawkins whose land was crossed by the tracks. Confusion with another stop named Haskins resulted in the name of the Hawkins station being changed to Ira. Following the naming of the rail stop, the surrounding community became known as Ira. The Ira Post Office sat across the tracks. (*PLHS*)

In 1883, Henry Willett Howe established a post office at Ira and became the first postmaster. In 1906, he retired. His daughter, Abby Sheppard, took over as postmistress until 1940 when the post office was moved. Henry's son, Frank Howe, shared a space in the post office. Frank operated a printing press. Abby is standing in the doorway of the post office. Henry Willet Howe is on her right. (*PLHS*)

In 1887, Frank Howe bought a small printing press. His business operated under the name of The F.R. Howe Printing Company. His press printed handbills, programs, lessons for schoolteachers, and little books containing school plays, which were shipped to public schools all over the country. Seen here, from left to right, are Edwin Howe, Abby Howe, Nina Danforth Howe, and Frank Howe. (*Nina Stanford*)

In 1940, the Ira Post Office moved its location into one room at the end of Gaylord Hine's apple barn. Hine was the postmaster until the office was officially closed in 1953. Here, the Akron Library Bookmobile makes a call at the post office. Pictured, from left to right, are Mr. Hastings, Doris Wetmore, Lucille Wyatt, Cynthia Wyatt, Marie Cranz, Ethel Hine, William Stauffer, Margot Jackson, and Judy Wyatt. (PLHS)

The Ira schoolhouse operated from 1853 to 1922 when it closed. A state mandate for centralized schools decreased student enrollment. Afterwards, students were driven in a school wagon from Ira to Bath to attend the Bath Central School. The school and lot were sold to Carl Cranz for $320. Later, he sold it to Elvin Roscoe Porch, a salesman for Perfection Stove Company in Cleveland, Ohio for $270. (PLHS)

James S. Hine was raised on a farm in Wauseon, Ohio and worked his way through Ohio State University. He became a professor of entomology. He was the zoologist of the Katmati Expedition for the first National Geographic expedition in 1918. In 1896, he married Abbie Parker, sister of Nettie Cranz. They had four children. Seen here, from left to right, are Vernon Hine, Abbie Hine, Dorothy Hine, and James Hine. (*PLHS*)

In 1907, Professor Hine purchased this apple farm in Ira. The family vacationed here in the summers until 1917. During their summer visits, Professor Hine improved the apple farm and collected insects in the fields for his entomology collections at Ohio State University. Today, the house is owned by the National Park Service. It still sits along Oak Hill Road and serves as a dormitory for summer interns. (*PLHS*)

This farm was established by the Hammond family in 1810 until they sold it to William Cranz in 1863. Following William's death in 1894, its ownership fell to his son, Eugene Cranz, until his death in 1952. Eugene's son, Harmon Cranz, took charge until he left the valley for Florida in the 1970s and the farm was acquired by the National Park Service. (*PLHS*)

Eugene Cranz was born in 1863 in Holmes County. He attended Lebanon Normal School and Ohio State University in preparation for teaching. After his father's death, he inherited the 164-acre farm and became involved in scientific agriculture. He was interested in conservation and saw his property recognized as a tree farm. (*PLHS*)

This is a photograph of Eugene Cranz standing in his southern field. Ira Cemetery is in the background. He remained active in the Grange his entire life and served at the state level. In 1893, he married Nettie Parker, and they raised six children. (*PHLS*)

Eugene's son, Harmon, attended Ohio State University and had a lifelong passion for aviation. He maintained an airplane, which he housed in the south barn. He constructed a runway that crossed the farmland and ran behind the neighboring Wetmore home. Navigating this runway was a considerable challenge even to the most experienced pilot. (*PLHS*)

(*above*) The Hale house was built by pioneer Jonathan Hale and his sons in the 1820s. It was passed down to his son Andrew Hale, then to his grandson C.O. Hale, and finally to his great granddaughter, Clara Belle Ritchie. She willed it to the Western Reserve Historical Society, and it now serves as an open-air museum. This photograph was taken when C.O. Hale owned the property, *c.* 1910. (*PLHS*)

(*right*) C.O. Hale was the third generation of the Hale family to live in the brick home. He was a well-educated gentleman. He attended Western Reserve Academy in Hudson and graduated from Oberlin School of Business in 1870. He was a leading citizen in Bath Township and served three terms as a Representative to the Ohio State Legislature for Summit County. (*PLHS*)

This is the village of Botzum, formerly known as Yellow Creek, Niles, and Buckeye. A large warehouse, store, rail stop, and a dozen houses made up the town. The store was run by John A.

This is a photograph of Mr. and Mrs. Conrad Botzum. Upon the death of his father, John George Botzum, Conrad Botzum inherited the family farm. He engaged in general

Botzum. Here, he sold groceries, lumber, dry goods, and livestock. John A. Botzum's store is to the left of the picture. The Valley Railway locomotive and station are to the right. (*Robert J. Botzum*)

farming and marketed wheat, corn, hogs, and calves. His brother, John A. Botzum ran the general store. (*CVNP*)

Although the post office was known as Buckeye, with the arrival of the railroad the depot was named Botzum after the town's most affluent family. (*PLHS*)

Like Boston and Everett, Botzum also had a covered bridge. This bridge stood on Bath Road near present-day Riverview Road and carried Bath Road over the Cuyahoga River. (*PLHS*)

Five

ENJOYING RECREATION
IN THE VALLEY

The tradition of recreational activity in the Cuyahoga Valley can be traced back to the mid to late 19th century. As the urban centers of Cleveland and Akron emerged, the Cuyahoga Valley served as a green oasis away from the increasingly industrialized urban landscape. As early as 1880, passengers on the Valley Railway were encouraged by a published guidebook to appreciate the bucolic beauty of the Cuyahoga Valley as their train ride carried them through the countryside. The Cleveland Academy of Art organized trips into the Cuyahoga Valley on the railroad to "capture the rare and tempting" beauty of the valley. Even today, the valley maintains a vibrant artistic community. The Ohio & Erie Canal also became a recreational resource, hosting leisurely boat rides for church groups and organizations through the pastoral landscape.

As the 20th century began, the tradition of recreational activity in the valley became firmly established. Parts of the towpath were utilized as roads for the new automobile, and carriage trails snaking through the countryside were being utilized by "recreational" drivers. Farmers responded to these visitors by selling their produce directly to these tourists from roadside stands along the country roads. Even the Hale family offered some rooms of their historic homestead for weekend retreats for regional industrialists such as Akron's F.A. Seiberling, who came to the valley to rejuvenate.

In 1917, the Cleveland Metropolitan Park District was formed and later became the Cleveland Metroparks. In early planning efforts, the Olmsted Brothers landscape architecture firm was hired to provide assistance in designing the new urban park system. Realizing that the automobile would forever change the way people utilized public spaces, the Olmsteds recommended a series of park "reservations" around the perimeter of Cleveland connected by parkways. The Olmsted plan formed the foundation for what is now known as "The Emerald Necklace." Reservations were established in the Cuyahoga Valley at Brecksville and Bedford with miles of trails and numerous picnic areas.

Created in 1921, the Akron Metropolitan Park District (AMPD) also benefited from the landscape designs of the Olmsted Brothers. Under the leadership of AMPD's first director, Harold S. Wagner, the park district retained the Olmsteds to prepare a report to help define the new park system. Again, the Olmsted Brothers focused on the scenic beauty of the Cuyahoga Valley, and their report recommended that "one or more routes be secured for pleasure drives" along the Ohio & Erie Canal and on the "brinks or part way up the sides of the valley." The report also identified specific areas such as Furnace Run and Sand Run for recreational uses.

With the creation of regional metropolitan park districts and public interest in preserving the natural beauty of the Cuyahoga Valley, the recreational potential of the valley was beginning to be realized.

The work relief programs of Franklin D. Roosevelt's New Deal had a profound impact on the recreational character of the Cuyahoga Valley. The 1930s saw three Civilian Conservation Corps (CCC) camps in the valley: Virginia Kendall, Sand Run, and Brecksville. The CCC built lakes, bath houses, shelters, picnic areas, and other structures that significantly advanced the valley's park infrastructure in a short amount of time. Soon thousands of park visitors were using facilities created by the CCC.

The valley also became a retreat for numerous organizations during the dawning of the 20th century. The Young Crusaders were organized at Akron's Church of Our Savior. During the summers of 1903 and 1904 the group held a summer camp at Hale Farm. By the 1920s, both the Boy Scouts and Girl Scouts established large camps in the Cuyahoga Valley, which are still in operation today.

Other smaller organizations and church groups also found the valley a good location for recreational activities. In 1937, the Phillis Wheatley Association founded Camp Mueller as a retreat for young African-American women from Cleveland. In 1949, the First United Methodist Church of Bedford established Camp Onlofte in Boston Township. The Volunteers of America also maintained a camp in Boston Township on Boston Mills Road. Throughout the 20th century, hundreds of children, many from urban areas, experienced what it was like to "camp in the country."

In the 1960s, local citizen groups and elected officials realized that the natural, historic, and scenic qualities of the Cuyahoga Valley were potentially in danger from unchecked development, and they organized in an effort to protect the valley's natural and cultural resources. The result of their collective efforts was the creation of Cuyahoga Valley National Recreation Area (renamed Cuyahoga Valley National Park in 2000) on December 27, 1974. As a result, thousands of valley acres have been protected from development. Moreover, Cuyahoga Valley National Park has embraced the recreational tradition of the valley and has established and maintains miles of trails including the 22-mile Ohio & Erie Canal Towpath Trail.

This is a photograph of the Virginia Kendall Park Winter Sports Center, *c.* 1940. (*PLHS*)

Beginning in 1883, The Cleveland Academy of Art published a catalogue of illustrations done by its students. The Academy's top students would go on "field trips" to hone their artistic skills. Trips were made to the Chautauqua Lake region, to encampments of the Cleveland Grays, and on a "sketching picnic" aboard the Valley Railway to Peninsula. The May 1883 issue, shown here, featured the drawings from Peninsula. (*PLHS*)

Among the 50 members of the Cleveland Academy of Art who rode the Valley Railway to Peninsula was artist Archibald M. Willard. An instructor at the Academy, Willard gained eternal fame from his painting *Spirit of '76* which is known the world over. In this sketch Willard portrays Lock 29 in Peninsula with Peck's Grocery at the lock and the original Moody and Thomas Mill in the background. (*PLHS*)

109

In 1895, the Akron, Bedford & Cleveland Railroad was built through Boston Township to connect Akron and Cleveland. One attraction along the route of this "interurban" was the Great Arch at Boston Ledges, a popular picnic area and site of revival shows. Due to the construction on New York Central Railroad, the Great Arch vanished. The rail company built directly through it. Today, the area is reached by way of the Bike and Hike Trail. (*PLHS*)

The Young Crusaders were organized at Akron's Church of Our Savior by its Rector George P. Atwater. During the summers of 1903 and 1904, the group held an organized summer camp at the Hale family farm on Oak Hill Road. In June of 1904 they took a trip to Washington, D.C., and were received by President Theodore Roosevelt. (*PLHS*)

110

Akron industrialist H. Karl Butler purchased a farm east of Peninsula in 1919. Butler, a member of George Atwater's congregation, and offered his farm to the Boy Scouts in 1923 as a site for Camp Manatoc. The Boy Scouts purchased additional land and opened a new Camp Manatoc in 1932. This photograph shows the main entrance off Truxell Road. (*PLHS*)

Construction began on the dining hall for the new Camp Manatoc in 1931. Constructed entirely of wormy chestnut milled on the site, the building was listed on the National Register of Historic Places in 1997. To make the building useable in cooler weather, the screens shown in this photograph were replaced with windows. Scouts dining inside sit on hickory chairs with caned seats at round maple tables. (*PLHS*)

Also constructed out of wormy chestnut, this building was the focal point of all aquatic activities at the new Camp Manatoc. The first floor housed boats and lifesaving equipment in the winter and changing rooms and showers during the summer. The lifeguards lived on the second floor and had a bird's eye view of the lake from the three-storey tower. Deemed unusable, this building was demolished in the 1980s. (*PLHS*)

The lake at the new Camp Manatoc was named Lake Marnoc and was created by damming up Salt Run. Truxell Road originally ran through the middle of the lakebed and was re-routed to the south. A larger lake named Lake Litchfield was built to the north by damming Ritchie Run. Deemed an "attractive nuisance" by the camp's insurance company, Lake Marnoc was drained in the 1980s. (*PLHS*)

This is a photograph of the rear view of the Manatoc gate in 1946. The farm in the background was replaced by Brandywine Country Club in 1964. The words on the gate are from the camp poem written by David Atwater, son of George Atwater, who founded the Young Crusaders camp at Hale Farm in 1903 and 1904. This photograph was taken by 30-year employee, Wes Bergdorf. (*PLHS*)

To meet projected increases in enrollment, the Boy Scouts purchased more acreage in 1957. This land was combined with the area of the original Camp Manatoc to form a new facility in 1962. The Scouts chose the name Camp Butler in honor of their benefactor. Camp Butler had no centralized dining hall and troops cooked their own meals. Haskell Run was dammed to create Lake Okchanya. (*PLHS*)

Girl Scouting organized in the Akron area in 1918. By 1924, a 35-acre camp on Yellow Creek was opened. Named Camp Chanote, this facility was on rented land and soon became obsolete. Goodyear founder Charles Seiberling located a 206-acre tract of land near the Boston Ledges and persuaded twelve other individuals to pledge $1,000 each towards its purchase. The new facility named Camp Ledgewood opened its gates in 1932. (GSWRC)

Many of the original buildings at Camp Ledgewood were relocated from Camp Chanote and reassembled. The infirmary tent was replaced in 1933 by this building constructed out of boards made from blighted chestnut trees. Over the years more land was purchased until Camp Ledgewood included over 600 acres. Modernized many times over the years, today Camp Ledgewood continues to proudly serve the Girl Scouts. (GSWRC)

Created in 1938 by the Phillis Wheatley Association, Camp Mueller occupies 200 acres along Akron-Peninsula Road in the former Northampton Township. The Phillis Wheatley Association was established in 1911 in Cleveland as the Working Girls Home Association by Jane Edna Harris to help unmarried black women. The association's namesake, Phillis Wheatley (1753–1784), was a slave educated by a Boston, Massachusetts family and acknowledged as the first African-American poet. (*PWA*)

Camp Mueller is named in honor of Ralph S. Mueller, Sr., founder of Cleveland's Mueller Electric Company, who assisted with the purchase of the campsite. The camp was organized in response to requests for more outdoor opportunities for inner-city families. Initially, Camp Mueller was limited to black women, but the organization's mission evolved to include all inner-city youngsters from challenged backgrounds. (*PWA*)

In 1949, the First United Methodist Church of Bedford founded Camp Onlofte. The 56-acre site situated between the Ohio Turnpike Bridge and Boston Mills Road was donated to the church by Ralph S. Mueller, Sr. The camp was improved with a dining hall, lodges, swimming pool, and other structures. The construction of the Interstate 271 bridges in 1966 cut through the center of Camp Onlofte. (FUMCB)

Built in 1953, the 100-acre Tamsin Park became a premier family campground and resort. A former house and general store were remodeled into the Indian Mill Gift Shop in 1969. An all-metal house moved from the Alside Plant in Cuyahoga Falls became the American Indian Art Hall of Fame in 1970. By 2003, the property laid idle awaiting annexation to Cuyahoga Falls and the construction of nearly 300 homes. (PLHS)

CCC camps were operated by the U.S. Army. Typically, each camp consisted of four to five barracks, separate latrines and showers, mess hall, recreation hall, administration building, officers' headquarters, and equipment garages. Notice the basketball hoop and volleyball net in the center court of the Virginia Kendall barracks. (*CVNP*)

In August 1933, Harold S. Wagner, Director-Secretary of the Akron Metropolitan Park District, applied to the National Park Service for the creation of a CCC camp at Virginia Kendall Park. The application was approved, and CCC Company 576 arrived by train in December 1933. The camp was located along the south side of Route 303 at the present location of Happy Days Visitor Center. (*CVNP*)

CCC camps usually consisted of 200 young men between the ages of 18 and 25 known as "juniors." Juniors were paid $30 a month, of which $25 was sent back to their families. CCC camps not only provided employment opportunities, but also gave vocational training and academic instruction to the enrollees. This photograph shows Virginia Kendall CCC Company 576 in 1934. (CVNP)

The creation and implementation of the CCC program involved multiple federal agencies and state and local governments. Virginia Kendall CCC Company 576 was a joint effort between the Akron Metropolitan Park District, State of Ohio, National Park Service, and the U.S. Army. Initially, the CCC was called Emergency Conservation Work, which is evident on this early park sign that Park Patrolman Howard Dittoe is standing by. (CVNP)

Included among the CCC enrollees were eight men called Local Experienced Men (LEMs). LEMs were considered enrollees but were hired from the local relief roll. Construction Foreman Roland E. Arnold was a LEM with Virginia Kendall Company 576. A master wood craftsman, Arnold instructed woodworking classes for junior enrollees. In this photograph, Arnold is framing the roof of the Octagon Shelter. (*CVNP*)

The first visitor-oriented project to take place at Virginia Kendall was the construction of the Ledges Shelter. Designed by Akron architect Albert H. Good in 1933, the shelter contained a covered picnic area with an enclosed section and was attached to a two-story building designed as the "caretaker's residence." The building was constructed of wormy chestnut and sandstone, both native materials to the surrounding Kendall property. (*CVNP*)

This *c.* 1936 aerial photograph of the Virginia Kendall Ledges area illustrates the landscape design of the CCC's architects. Shelters, privies, and parking lots boarder large, open lawns called playsteads. Notice the large outcropping of Sharon Conglomerate that constitutes the Ledges Overlook in the foreground. (*CVNP*)

In this 1936 photograph, CCC workmen are constructing the stone façade of the bath house at Virginia Kendall Lake. Opening in 1937, the bath house supported lake activities. In the summer, the bath house served as the dressing and shower area, and attendants checked clothing from behind the counter. In the winter, the bath house was used as a shelter for ice skaters. (*CVNP*)

Completed by the CCC in 1935, 13-acre Virginia Kendall Lake was built by damming Salt Run. The lake included a 100-foot earthen fishing pier extending from its south shore. A bath house and sandy beaches also lined the south shore. Almost immediately, the lake became a popular recreation venue attracting thousands of visitors a year both in summer and winter. (*CVNP*)

During the winter of 1935–1936, the CCC built a single toboggan slide on the southeastern side of Kendall Lake. The toboggan run utilized a natural hill with the slope made steeper by raising the chute off of the ground with wooden supports. A second chute was added the following winter. In 1939, the toboggan runs were permanently relocated to the extreme southeast end of the lake. (*CVNP*)

In 1938, the CCC began their last project at Virginia Kendall Park, the construction of the Happy Days Camp. The camp was built on the former site of CCC Company 576 on Route 303. Opening in 1939, the building became the permanent overnight campgrounds for the Akron Board of Education and Recreation Commission's summer playground program that was begun in 1931. (CVNP)

The CCC also built a bath house and lake at Furnace Run Reservation. CCC work began at Furnace Run in 1936 with the dam and lake being completed three years later. Completed in March 1941, the Furnace Run Bath House opened for public use on July 4, 1941. (CVNP)

The CCC operated two tree nurseries in the Cuyahoga Valley during the 1930s. One of the nurseries was located at Everett south of Everett Road and west of Riverview Road on part of a 234-acre tract owned by the Akron Metropolitan Park District. Elmer Baker, the nursery foreman, directed 47 CCC enrollees assigned to the site. (*CVNP*)

In April 1934, the Cleveland Stone Company donated a 41-acre quarry near Lock 28 (Deep Lock) to the Akron Metropolitan Park District. The CCC mined Deep Lock Quarry for sandstone to be used in construction projects at Virginia Kendall Park. This 1936 photograph shows CCC workers scoring and cutting sandstone blocks. Today, the quarry is a park managed by the Metro Parks, Serving Summit County. (*CVNP*)

Built in 1973 on a 300-acre site at the intersection of Route 303 and Interstate 271, the Richfield Coliseum was home to the Cleveland Cavaliers, Cleveland Barons, and other professional sports teams. The Coliseum was constructed at a cost of approximately $36 million, and its structural footprint occupied nearly six acres. The Coliseum closed in 1994 after only 20 years in operation. The building was razed in 1999. (*CVNP*)

From 1974 to 1993, when the Ringing Bros. Barnum & Bailey Circus came to town people lined route 303 to catch a glimpse of the "Animal Walk" from the Peninsula depot to the Richfield Coliseum where they performed. Schools were let out early so children could view the spectacular parade of circus animals, clowns, and trainers. The last "walk" was in 1993 as the Coliseum closed in 1994. (*PLHS*)

Boston Mills Ski Resort opened December 1963 with two slopes for beginners, five for intermediates, and one for experts. A ski shop, cafeteria, and bar are housed in a chalet style lodge with glass fronts facing the ski runs. A ski school provides lessons to individuals and school groups. Beginning in 1972, the Akron Society of Artists organized the nationally known Boston Mills Art Festival which is held every summer. (*PLHS*)

Brandywine Ski Resort, the sister ski resort to Boston Mills, is located on Highland Road just east of Jaite. It also opened in December of 1963. Brandywine offers a ski school, ski equipment rental, restaurant and bar area housed in similar chalet lodges. During the summer months, neighboring Dover Lake Park is the site of numerous water rides and a small amusement park. (*PLHS*)

Located in the former Northampton Township five miles north of Akron, Blossom Music Center is the summer home of the world renowned Cleveland Orchestra. It opened to the public, July 1968. Patrons enjoy not only orchestra concerts but also musical concerts of all genres, seated on grassy slopes or under the fan shaped pavilion. In 2003, Blossom underwent a $14 Million renovation. (*R. Todd Mayer*)

Once the location of both a stone quarry that shipped material worldwide and the deepest lock on the Ohio & Erie Canal, Deep Lock Quarry Park originated in 1934 when the Cleveland Stone Company donated 41 acres to the Akron Metropolitan Park District. During the 1960s, an additional 150 acres were added to the park. In this photo park naturalist Bert Szabo is discussing how stone was quarried. (*PLHS*)

In 1937, the Civilian Conservation Corps began construction on the Brecksville Trailside Museum. Works Progress Administration workers eventually completed the construction of the rustic museum in 1939. The building is now the Cleveland Metroparks' Brecksville Nature Center. (*CMP*)

Opening in 1993, the 22-mile Ohio & Erie Canal Towpath Trail has become a premier attraction at Cuyahoga Valley National Park with over a million visitors a year using the multipurpose trail. (*Tom Jones*)

In the mid-1970s, the Cuyahoga Valley Preservation and Scenic Railway Association began offering train excursions through Cuyahoga Valley National Park on what was known as the Cuyahoga Valley Line. The railroad utilized the historic alignment of the Valley Railway. In 1994, the railroad reorganized as Cuyahoga Valley Scenic Railroad. Today, the line continues the tradition of tourism and recreation through Cuyahoga Valley, transporting over 100,000 passengers a year. (*Tom Jones*)

CPSIA information can be obtained
at www.ICGtesting.com
Printed in the USA
LVHW060119080520
655008LV00001B/40